SOFTBALL

SOFTBALL: PITCHING

BARBARA BONNEY

The Rourke Corporation, Inc.
Vero Beach, Florida 32964

Barbara Bonney is a librarian and freelance writer in Cincinnati, Ohio. Besides enjoying research and words, she likes creating with food and fabrics. She has two children.

PHOTO CREDITS:
All photos © Tony Gray except; © East Coast Studios: pages 4, 12

EDITORIAL SERVICES:
Susan Albury

Library of Congress Cataloging-in-Publication Data

Bonney, Barbara, 1955-
    Softball—pitching / by Barbara Bonney.
       p. cm. — (Softball)
    Includes index
    Summary: Mentions the importance of the pitcher in softball and describes pitching techniques and various kinds of pitches.
    ISBN 0-86593-478-9
    1. Pitching (Softball)—Juvenile literature. [1. Pitching (Softball)
2. Softball.] I. Title. II. Series: Bonney, Barbara, 1955- Softball.
GV881.4.P57B66 1998
796.357'22—dc21

                                                    98–11088
                                                        CIP
                                                         AC

Printed in the USA

TABLE OF CONTENTS

RESPONSIBILITIES

Winning or losing a fast-pitch softball game often centers on the pitcher. The pitcher's skill in throwing **strikes** (STRYKS) is important in keeping the other team's score low. A pitcher should also be able to field balls and **relay** (REE lay) throws since so many plays come through the **infield** (IN feeld). Just as important as those skills is the need for the pitcher to have good **concentration** (kon sen TRAY shun) on the game and be able to ignore jeers from others. To pitch a whole game, pitchers must be physically fit and have strong legs, back, and arms.

A professional softball pitcher, Eddie Feigner, struck out 100,468 batters which is 20 times more than Nolan Ryan's total of 4,577. Eddie also pitched 216 perfect games.

Fielding balls in the infield is another responsibility of a pitcher.

GRIP

Pitchers who are very experienced have a different grip for every kind of pitch, but they start with a basic grip. The ball is held by fingers on one side and thumb on the other side.

Grip the ball without letting it touch the palm.

Softball pitches are always underhand.

Younger players will need to use all four fingers, but older and larger players might use three or two fingers to grip. Since the pitch is made underhand, the fingers will be on the bottom of the ball when it is pitched. Only the fingers and thumb should touch the ball, never the palm.

STANCE AND PRESENTATION

Before every pitch, the pitcher must stand in position on the pitcher's plate. Both feet must be touching the plate, but one can be ahead of the other. Shoulders must be lined up with first and third bases and the pitcher must be facing the batter. The ball is held inside the glove with the pitching hand. All pitchers must **present** (pree ZENT) the ball before a windup. This means their hands are held together at waist height for at least one second and not more than 20 seconds before taking away one hand to pitch.

Presentation of the ball comes before every softball pitch.

SEQUENCE

Every pitch has an order of movements, or sequence. The movements are different for different types of pitches, but the order stays the same.

First is the windup, which is the preparation for the pitch. A windup helps the ball's speed and **control** (kun TROHL). Any windup can be used but it must not be stopped, reversed, or faked.

The next part of the pitch is the delivery, which is when the ball is released. At the same time, the pitcher takes a step with the foot that was behind.

The last part is the follow-through. The ball is not involved, but the arm should continue to swing up in a smooth motion.

A pitch puts the ball into play.

This pitcher is winding up before releasing the ball.

SLINGSHOT

The slingshot is a type of windup used in fast-pitch softball. In it, the arm acts as a sort of slingshot for the ball, pitching it at a high speed. The pitching arm is first brought back slowly until it is above and behind the head.

The power of a slingshot windup comes from the pitching arm and the back leg.

A fast-pitch ball is released at knee level.

At the same time, the leg is stretched out in front when the ball is at its peak. Then the leg steps down just before the arm is snapped forward, releasing the ball at about knee level. A good push from the stepping leg against the pitcher's plate can add force to the pitch. This windup is easier to learn for beginning pitchers.

WINDMILL

Another type of fast-pitch windup is the windmill. After presenting the ball, both arms move upward and forward. The leg stretches forward while the pitching arm continues to move upward and over the head. The arm circles around like a windmill turning. When the arm is on the downswing, near the knee, the front leg steps down, the wrist snaps and the ball is released. The arm follows through in a straight path and usually the back foot lifts off of the pitcher's plate.

A good pitcher knows each batter's likes and dislikes for pitches and uses this in planning pitches.

The pitching arm circles like a windmill.

14

FAST-PITCH

Fast-pitch rules are a little different from slow-pitch rules. In fast-pitch, there are nine players, and bunts and **stealing** (STEE ling) are allowed. The pitch is underhand but very fast with a low **arc** (ARK), almost straight. Pitchers must concentrate on speed and aim to get strikes. The pitch is full of power and the ball is whipped toward the catcher. Fast-pitch is harder and more complex than slow-pitch, and the game depends more on the pitcher.

The pitch is kept lower in fast-pitch softball.

SLOW-PITCH

Slow-pitch softball allows ten players on each team with the tenth position added as a short outfielder. Bunting and stealing are not permitted in slow-pitch games. The pitching is the main difference. A slow-pitch must have a high arc, usually between six and 12 feet (1.83 and 3.66 meters).

Slow-pitch softball requires a gentler, higher pitch.

Slow-pitched balls are hard to hit because they come in on an arc.

How high the arc is depends on which organization's rules the game is played under. The pitcher does not have to throw strikes. Instead, the high slow arc makes the ball hard to hit. The pitches are delivered in an easy, half-circle underhand sweep and the ball is tossed rather than whipped.

DRILLS

The movement of a pitch should be practiced before the aim is practiced. A player alone can watch the arm movement in a mirror or another player can help by guiding the pitching hand through the windup. A beginning pitcher too focused on where the ball is going can be blindfolded in order to concentrate on the right movements.

Drills can include pitching against a strike rectangle chalked on a wall, pitching hard against a wall without caring about aim, or pitching into a bucket (slow-pitch).

Joan Joyce, the top female softball pitcher of all time, pitched a fastball at 100 m.p.h. In 1962 she pitched 40 balls to Ted Williams and he hit just two of them.

This pitcher is practicing her slow pitch.

GLOSSARY

arc (ARK) — curve

concentration (kon sen TRAY shun) — focusing on one thought or goal

control (kun TROHL) — to direct something and not let it be unguided

infield (IN feeld) — the area around the bases and pitcher

present (pree ZENT) — to show the ball so everyone can see it

relay (REE lay) — returning the ball in short fast throws between several players rather than throwing the ball a very long distance

stealing (STEE ling) — to go to the next base during the pitch instead of after the pitch is released

strike (STRYK) — a pitch that is swung at and missed or hit into foul territory; also a pitch thrown into the strike zone and not swung at

Pitching takes good concentration.

INDEX

FURTHER READING

Find out more about softball with these helpful books and information sites:
Elliott, Jill & Martha Ewing, eds. *Youth Softball: A Complete Handbook.* printed by Brown & Benchmark, 1992
Rookie Coaches Softball Guide/American Sport Education Program. Human Kinetics Publishers, Inc., 1992
Cohen, Neil, ed. *The Everything You Wanted to Know About Sports Encyclopedia.* Bantam Books, 1994
Boehm, David A., editor-in-chief. *Guinness Sports Record Book 1990-91.* Sterling Publishing Co., Inc. 1990

on the internet at
www.softball.com/othrlink.htm (links to organizations, equipment manufacturers, teams, etc)